I0434431

The Tao of George W. Bush

The Tao of George W. Bush

Ed Bremson

iUniverse, Inc.
New York Lincoln Shanghai

The Tao of George W. Bush

All Rights Reserved © 2003 by Ed Bremson

No part of this book may be reproduced or transmitted in any form or by any means, graphic, electronic, or mechanical, including photocopying, recording, taping, or by any information storage retrieval system, without the written permission of the publisher.

iUniverse, Inc.

For information address:
iUniverse, Inc.
2021 Pine Lake Road, Suite 100
Lincoln, NE 68512
www.iuniverse.com

ISBN: 0-595-29883-4

Printed in the United States of America

For Ma Ma, Mother, and Betty Jean

Preface

This is not a book of quotations by George W. Bush. Rather, it is intended to illustrate and parody how the author imagines the President might react to or interpret the *Tao Te Ching* if he were to read it. This is therefore a work of the imagination. It is not just a book about George W. Bush, however. It is also an authentic, somewhat tongue-in-cheek reading of the *Tao Te Ching*. The reader would benefit (i.e. gain more understanding) by becoming better acquainted with the ideas of both George W. Bush and the *Tao Te Ching*.

During the course of writing this work I consulted the 1891 James Legge translation of the *Tao Te Ching*. It is a rather antiquated translation, and my work owes much of its style to it. The italicized passages in this book were taken directly from the *Tao Te Ching*, and from Mr. Legge's commentary. The numbering scheme corresponds to the numbered sections of the *Tao Te Ching*. The reader can refer to the original in order to better understand the context of the excerpts.

I tried not to be too disrespectful to George W. Bush or to the *Tao Te Ching*.

Introduction

President George W. Bush attended the Asia Pacific Economic Cooperation (APEC) summit in October of 2003. In preparation for that trip he wanted to try and understand the Oriental mind. He therefore took a copy of the *Tao Te Ching* on vacation with him in August. He thought reading that book would help. Well, a day turned into a week, and a week turned into a month. When his vacation was finally over, he had finished reading and making notes on the *Tao Te Ching*. These notes were collected by Secretary of State Powell, and they form the text of the book before you now, unedited and direct from the pencil of the President.

1

Where the Mystery is deepest is the gate of all that is subtle and wonderful.

How now
Mysterious Tao?
What's in a name?
Originator of heaven and earth
Or the Mother of all things?
Mother of all things sounds
Too much like Saddam Hussein talking.
We've looked for his butt
All over heaven and earth.
Him and Osama bin Laden.
I bet they changed their names
And are hiding in some hole somewhere.
Snakes sometimes hide in holes.
In Texas we kill snakes.
No mystery in that.

2

All know the beauty of the beautiful, and in doing so know what ugliness is.

Knowing sorrow and loss
We are given the ideas of joy and gain.
Knowing defeat and death
We are given the ideas of victory and life,
And more defeat and death,
But for the evildoers.
Not for us.

The ideas of existence
And non-existence
Give birth to each other:
Existence for us,
Non-existence for the terrorists.
For all infinite justice,
Let it be so.

The sage manages affairs
Without doing anything,
And conveys his instructions
Without the use of speech.
I am a sage.

3

The sage constantly tries to keep the people without knowledge and without desire.

We must keep the people at rest.
Restless people are not happy voters.
We must keep them happy.
Empty their minds,
Fill their bellies,
Weaken their wills,
Strengthen their bones,
Give them a tax cut.
Give them another tax cut.
After all, it's not my money.
I get a big tax cut too
In my blind trust.

Sages don't hire really smart people
To work for them.
They don't hire people who disagree with them.
Or they get rid of them if they do.

The sage tries to keep people
Without knowledge and desire.
Too much knowledge and desire
And the sage might be out of
A job in 2004.

4

The Tao is like the emptiness of a vessel.

> Some people want to talk
> About the emptiness of a vessel.
> I don't understand what they mean.
> I'd rather talk about something else.

5

Heaven and earth do not act from any wish to be benevolent; they deal with things as the dogs of grass are dealt with.

Sages don't do things to be nice.
They do things because they're sages,
And because they've got it all figured out.

And what's all this about
The dogs of grass?
I like dogs
And I like grass.
At least I used to in college.
Sages treat people like dogs.
It says so in the Tao.
I don't have a problem with that.
As I said, I like dogs,
And I treat them pretty darn good.

6

The valley spirit dies not, aye the same; the female mystery thus we do name.

> I have women who work for me.
> I don't understand any of them.
> There's something mysterious
> About a woman.
> But they're good to have around
> Sometimes.

7

Heaven is long-enduring and earth continues long because they do not live for themselves.

> The world's oil
> Will last forever,
> Or at least until 2008 which,
> Politically, is the same thing.
>
> Unselfishness has
> Its own rewards:
> Those who donate
> Large sums to my
> Re-election campaign
> Will benefit from
> My next tax cut.

8

The excellence of a residence is in the suitability of the place.

The best house is in
The best place, like Crawford, Texas.
Not Washington, D. C.,
Where you can't even
See the stars at night.
It's important to see the stars.
It keeps your mind peaceful.
There is a great deal of
Virtue in that.

The best times are
Those spent in Crawford,
Like August, the whole month,
Working on the ranch
And then going on the road
To raise money.

9

When one's work is done, and one's name is distinguished, to withdraw into obscurity is the way of Heaven.

> I'd like to withdraw
> Into obscurity
> And be like I was before;
> But I have more taxes to cut,
> More deficits to raise,
> More wars to fight,
> More elections to win,
> And if I'm lucky
> I get to appoint some justices
> To the U. S. Supreme Court.
> That's worth sticking around for,
> Especially if I need their votes
> In the next election.

10

In loving the people and ruling the state, cannot he proceed without any purpose of action?

> In doing my job, I don't have to appear
> As if I have any purpose of action at all.
> It says so in the Tao.
> I can also appear
> To be without knowledge sometimes
> If I want to,
> And sometimes I want to.
> You just don't understand
> Such mysterious things,
> But I do,
> So get off my back.
> I'm the one who's ruling the state,
> Or the country,
> Which is the same thing.

11

Clay is fashioned into vessels; but it is on their hollowness that their use depends.

Empty space can be very useful.
A pot is useful because it is empty.
A door is useful when it is open.
A room depends on the empty space within
To be a room.
Remember that
The next time you're
Criticizing me.

12

The sage seeks to satisfy the craving of the belly, and not the longing of the eyes.

It is OK to eat all you want.
In fact it is necessary
For a growing, healthy economy.
In the words of JFK,
Ask what you cannot eat
For your country.
Also, ask what you can eat
For your country.
You cannot eat French cheese
And French wine.
You can eat all things
American, in large quantities.
What better for the world's
Only superpower than
Everything and everyone
Supersized?

13

Favor and grace would seem equally to be feared.

Those who have lots of things
Could end up losing them.
This leads to worry and fear.
That is the way of the Tao.

If you don't have anything,
You can't lose anything,
And there is no cause
To worry.

For example, there is a bright side
To not having a job.
You can't lose something
That you don't have.

So those who are unemployed,
Or living in poverty,
Cheer up.
Things can't get any worse,
Unless you die,
And don't worry
We won't kill you.

14

We look at it, and we do not see it, and we call its name 'Equable.'

Many things cannot be
Seen or heard or
Held in your hand.
Like the deficit:
You can't see that;
But a tax cut,
You can hold that
In your hand.
You can spend it
To help your family
Or just to buy something.
I think people would rather
Concentrate on what they can
Hold in their hand
Instead of on what
May or may not
Be in the bush.

15

Who can make the muddy water clear? Let it be still and it will gradually become clear. The skillful masters of old comprehended the mysteries of the Tao.

Anyone can muddy the water.
Who can leave it alone
And let it become clear?
Anyone can stir up
Restlessness and impatience.
Who among us can wait?
My tax cuts will
Stimulate the economy
And improve the lives
Of our citizens.
Many wise men of old
Agree with me on this.
Listen to the wise men.
Quiet your mind.
In fact, don't think about
Anything at all.
It works for me.

16

All things go through their processes of activity, and then return to their original state.

Cycles.
Sometimes you're up,
Sometimes you're down.
They're all just cycles.
That's why I don't
Pay any attention
To polls.
It's where you end up
That counts.
In 2000 I ended up
On top.

The economy?
They're all cycles too.
Five year business cycles;
Stock market, bond market,
Housing starts.
There's only so much
You can do about
Any of that.
But I'm doing what I can
To stimulate the economy.
And it's where all that ends up
That really counts;
Whether, like my daddy,
I get credit for it
Or not.

17

In antiquity the people did not know their rulers.

Sometimes the people
Love their leaders.
Sometimes they
Fear them or despise them.
I know a lot of people despise me,
Some even in the Middle East,
But they can't vote
So what do I care?

18

When the Great Tao ceased to be observed, benevolence and righteousness came into vogue.

> Benevolence and righteousness
> Have not always been in vogue.
> Sometimes there was hypocrisy.
> Sometimes there was dissonance,
> Like when the Dixie Chicks
> Said those things about me.
> They should be glad
> I'm so benevolent.

19

If we could renounce our sageness and discard our wisdom, it would be better for the people.

> I can't renounce my sageness
> Or discard my wisdom.
> I wish I could.
> I can't renounce
> My benevolence
> Or discard my righteousness.
> I've got a job to do
> And I'm going to do it.
> Those who scheme for gain,
> As well as the hypocrites
> Should be ashamed of themselves.
> No, I'm talking about the Democrats.

20

When we renounce learning we have no troubles.

> My mind may be that of a stupid man.
> I may be in a state of chaos.
> Ordinary men may seem brilliant,
> While I may seem dull and confused.
> But who's the President of the United States?
> Come on and say it:
> George W. Bush.

21

The grandest forms of active force come from the Tao, their only source.

> The grandest forms of active force
> Come not from Tao, their only source,
> But from Army, Navy,
> Marines, Air Force;
> Brave men and women in the course
> Of daily duties every one,
> Fighting battles that must be won,
> To make the world a safer place
> For you, me, and the whole human race.
> Even the Arabs.

22

He whose desires are few, gets them; he whose desires are many goes astray.

My desires are few.
All I want is
87 billion dollars
For the war in Iraq,
Etc.

That could be a lesson
To you all:
Don't go astray.
Be humble and distinguished.
Be a sage like me.

23

A violent wind does not last for a whole morning; a sudden rain does not last for a whole day.

When it rains it pours.
An ill wind,
Well, something, something.
The fire of Heaven and Earth
Rains down upon the evildoers.
All's right with the world.
And if it's not,
I'll fix it.

24

He who stands on his tiptoes does not stand firm. He who displays himself does not shine. He who vaunts himself does not find his merit acknowledged.

Who stands on tiptoes anyway?
Women, some types of men,
Sometimes people changing light bulbs.
I want an order going out
To all the troops:
"No standing on tiptoes!"
Why, you might as well wear
Tutus and toe shoes.
No one respects someone on tiptoes.

Also, you can't display yourself,
At least not in public,
Or vaunt yourself.
I don't even know what that means
But it doesn't sound good.
Everybody understand?
Shape up or ship out.

25

Heaven is great. Earth is great.

The American people are great.
They elected me.
Even though I didn't get
The most actual votes,
I got the ones that counted most.

The people deserve
A President like me.
Why, I never could work
Those punch card ballots either.
So I understand
Where you're coming from.
And I understand
Where you're going.
Let's go there together.
Wait a minute,
Do I go two blocks this way
And turn right?
Or is it left?

26

Gravity is the root of lightness; stillness the ruler of movement.

What goes up must come down.
It's called gravity,
Like with the bombs
Falling over Iraq.
It's that way, I think,
With the stock market too.
It's not my fault
That so many people
Lost money in their 401k's.

I know I haven't said much lately
About investing Social Security
In the stock market.
That doesn't mean I think
It's a bad idea.
I've just been busy trying to prove that,
Unlike my father,
I can win a war
And still be re-elected President.

27

The skillful traveler leaves no traces of his wheels or footsteps.

The skillful President,
Like Teddy Roosevelt said,
Walks softly and
Carries a big stick.
I've got the biggest stick
Any President ever had,
And I'm not afraid to use it.
Just ask the people of
Afghanistan and Iraq.

The terrorists may have caught us
With our pants down,
But we've pulled them up
And buckled our belt.
They can't see our stick,
But they'd better watch out.
They're on our list,
And they know
Which list
I'm talking about.

28

He who knows how white attracts,
Yet always stays within black's shade,
In the unchanging excellence arrayed,
Return to man's first state has made.

I think I'd like to be called
"Your Excellecy."
Yeah, that has a good ring to it.
I like it when they play
"Hail to the Chief."
They could play that,
And then announce,
"His Excellency, George W. Bush."
Yeah, that sounds good.
Maybe I should do
A Presidential Proclamation.
Where are those Proclamation forms
Anyway?

29

If anyone should wish to get the kingdom for himself, I see that he will not succeed.

The Tao says I'm going to win
The next election.
All those Democrats
Who want my job
"Will not succeed."
Maybe after the election
I'll get a throne
For the TV room.
I think I'd like
To watch the Super Bowl
While sitting on a throne,
Eating a bag of pretzels.
I also wouldn't mind
Having a court jester.

30

A skillful commander strikes a decisive blow and stops. He does not dare to assert and complete his mastery.

I don't know how
These people ever won
Any wars way back then.
Some of their ideas
Are plainly stupid.
But who knows,
Maybe it's because
Of the weapons they had?
You can't do much with
Bows and arrows,
Swords or stones.
Give them a couple of
Cruise missiles,
A B1 bomber;
Keep the nuclear option
On the table
And they'd change their tune.
War may be contrary to
The spirit of the Tao,
But let me know
When the Tao
Finds Osama bin Laden.

31

Weapons, however beautiful, are instruments of evil omen, hateful.

I know I'm not going to convert
To Taoism any time soon.
They're against war,
And I've already won two of them.
I might even wage a few more
Before I leave office.
And those Taoists
Are probably against
Capital punishment too.
No, I'll stay with Christianity.
That way I get to have
More fun.

32

If a leader could hold onto the Tao, everyone would submit themselves to him.

Everyone submits themselves
To me as it is.
I've got the bombs, the planes
And the fighting men.
Who's going to stand in my way?
Oh, I know France
Does some grumbling
Every now and then,
But if push came to shove,
We'd be doing all
The pushing and shoving.
They'd throw a hunk of cheese
And we'd throw a hand grenade.
Who needs the Tao
When I've got a god-awful big
Military budget?

33

He who does not fail in the requirements of his position will continue long.

Now that's more like it.
I've done a good job.
I've won two wars
And given two tax cuts.
So again, according to the Tao,
I should be re-elected in 2004.
Sometimes I like what
The Tao has to say
And sometimes I don't.
I like this.

34

The influence of the Tao is felt in the vegetable world.

The Tao may be OK
In the vegetable world,
But in the world of
Bombs and missiles,
Terrorists, armies
And planes
You'd better let me
Be in charge.

Hold on!
I just remembered that
Monsanto has to be in charge
Of the vegetable world.
I guess that leaves the Tao out.

35

The benevolence of the Tao is inexhaustible.

The benevolence of
The American people
Is inexhaustible.
So are our abilities.
In this way
The Tao is a lot like we are.
But the truth is,
The Tao could learn
Some things from us:
Our resourcefulness,
Our patience,
Our resolve.
How to make a
Peanut butter and jelly sandwich.
How to grill a hot dog.
How to set off fireworks on holidays.
Boy! The good old
American Way.

36

Instruments for the profit of the state should not be shown to the people.

The Tao says that a leader
Can keep the people
In a state of simplicity
And ignorance.
It also says
I don't have to tell
Anybody everything about
What the government does
With its money.
I don't always agree
With the Tao,
But this is one time when
I do.

37

The exercise of government should be according to the Tao, doing without doing, governing without government.

I'm all for smaller, simpler government
And I don't think Washington
Has all the answers.
I think Washington needs
To get out of the lives of more people
Especially corporate CEOs,
Who are the backbone
Of our economy,
As are everyday
Hard working people.
No, Washington needs
To get after the terrorists.
Hunt them down,
Pin them down,
Neutralize them.
Ha, ha, I like that word:
Neutralize.

38

The great man dwells with the fruit and not with the flower.

Flowers are pretty,
But fruit is pretty too
If you think about it.
Besides, you can eat fruit.
It tastes good
And it's good for you
Although sometimes
It may be a little messy.
Who wants to eat flowers?
Maybe Flower Children,
Not me.

39

They do not wish to show themselves elegant-looking as jade, but prefer to be coarse-looking as an ordinary stone.

You may prefer
To be coarse-looking
As an ordinary stone.
I prefer to look like jade.
Wait a minute.
Jade is green, right?
OK, then, I'd rather be a ruby.
No, it's "better dead than red"
Isn't it?
What about a sapphire?
Blue? Maybe not.
Oh, I've got it:
I'd like to be a diamond.
Diamonds are
Somebody's best friend
Aren't they?
I need all the votes
I can get.

40

The movement of the Tao by contraries proceeds.

Republicans and Democrats
Are contrary to each other.
Sometimes it's hard
To get anything done.
When we do get things done,
Like a law passed,
Things like that,
It is not because
Of this contrariness.
It's because we have
More votes then they do.
So help me out in 2004.
Send more Republicans
To Congress.
I appreciate it.
(This message paid for by
Really rich people ·
Getting richer while
I'm in office.)

41

Scholars laugh greatly at the Tao. If not, it would not be worthy to be called the Tao.

I'm glad I'm not
The only one
Who feels like
Laughing at the Tao.

42

The Tao made One; One made Two; Two made Three; Three made All Things.

> You know, I don't feel too bad
> For not understanding
> All this stuff.
> Even the guy who
> Translated it and
> Wrote the commentary
> Is just as baffled
> As I am sometimes.
> What's that they say
> About the Oriental mind?
> Inscrutable?
> Yeah.

43

The softest thing in the world dashes against and overcomes the hardest.

> I would have thought
> That would be
> The other way around,
> With hard things
> Dashing against soft things.
> At least that's
> The way it works
> Where I come from.
> Get my drift?

44

Of life or wealth, which is more dear?

Sometimes the Tao
Sinks into absurdity.
No one wants to lose his life.
All the stock options
In the world are not
Worth losing your life.
Of course, there is such a thing
As martyrs.
Some people do want to die,
Like those hijacking evildoers,
Or Osama bin Laden.
Well, in some instances
I'd be happy to oblige them.
I sent a lot of men
To their deaths
When I was in Texas.
I'll be happy to do the same
In Washington, D. C.
Just ask Timothy McVeigh.

45

Do thou what's straight
Still crooked deem;
Thy greatest art still stupid seem,
And eloquence a stammering scream.

I never liked Shakespeare, you know.
All that playing around with words,
Acting cute, just seemed stupid to me,
Made me want to scream.
I couldn't even understand
What he was talking about half the time.

This passage seems like MS:
More of the same.
Well, I'm a man of plain talk
And few words.
No, wait a minute,
That's John McCain.
Well anyway, I don't like
All this flowery talk.
It's for flower children,
Not for me.

46

There is no guilt greater than to sanction ambition.

> Some of this is getting to be
> Like a broken record.
> OK, so according to the Tao
> You're not supposed
> To want anything.
> Well, just how far has that
> Gotten the Chinese,
> Huh?
> More than a billion people,
> Poverty, problems at home;
> And who's number one
> In the world,
> Huh?
> We're number one!
> We're number one!

47

Without going outside his door, one understands all that takes place under the sky.

This passage sounds like
They're talking about
The Weather Channel.
But they didn't have
TVs back then.
Do they have TVs now?
Probably, but I doubt that
The peasants have one.
They have a lot of
Peasants over there.
If China would ever get its
Act together, we could
Do some business with them.
We could sell them TVs,
Cable, satellite dishes.
Then they could check out
The Weather Channel
And find out what's
Really going on
Under the sky.

48

He who devotes himself to the Tao seeks from day to day to diminish his doing.

OK, first they say
You're supposed to
Want nothing.
Then they say
You're supposed to
Do nothing.
No wonder the Chinese economy
Is in the shape it is.
That's not the way it works
In this country.
We want a lot
And we'll do almost
Anything to get it,
Especially when it comes to
Things like oil.

49

To those who are not good to me, I am also good.

This reminds me
Of the Christian idea
Of turning the other cheek,
And that's all well and good,
But when the evildoers
Smite us on one cheek,
I think it is OK
For us to smite them back.
That's the only way
We can get them to stop
Doing evil.

50

The rhinoceros finds no place in him into which to thrust his horn.

> You say that a rhinoceros
> Can't hurt you?
> That's foolish.
> If a rhinoceros
> Comes running after you,
> You'd better take
> Evasive action
> Or kill him.
> I didn't say to run.
> In this country
> We never run.

51

All things without exception honor the Tao and exalt its outflowing operation.

Now it sounds like
They're talking about God,
You know like in the hymn
"Praise God from whom
All blessings flow."
If that's true,
Then I can understand it
A lot better.
In any case,
I'm sure the Tao
Is on our side
In the war against terror.

52

Who uses well his light,
Reverting to its source so bright,
Will from his body ward all blight,
And hides the unchanging from men's sight.

> Once again the translator
> And commentator admits that
> Even he doesn't understand
> One of these passages.
> Great. Now I don't feel so alone,
> Or dumb.
> Besides, maybe it's the Tao
> That's dumb.
> Did you ever think of that?

53

If I were suddenly to be put into a position to conduct a government according to the Great Tao, I should be most afraid of a boastful display.

Should I be "most afraid
Of a boastful display?"
Well, I've often talked of humility,
So I don't plan to be boastful.
Should I carry a sharp sword?
Well I'm going to.
I don't care what the Tao says.
I'm a compassionate guy,
But that only goes so far.
Compassion in the face of evil
Is evil.
I really believe that.

54

Tao when nursed within one's self,
His vigor will make true;
And where the family it rules,
What riches will accrue.

OK, first the Tao says
You're not supposed
To want anything.
Now is promises that
"riches will accrue"
If you let it rule your family.
Then it says you'll thrive
And have good fortune.
It doesn't sound to me
Much different than
The promises of some politicians,
"Pie in the sky," so to speak.
Well, I promised tax cuts
And you got tax cuts.
You got to hold them
In your hands.
You could have bought
A lot of pie with them.

55

Poisonous insects will not sting him; fierce beasts will not seize him; birds of prey will not strike him.

> If anyone thinks
> He's safe from
> Poisonous insects,
> Fierce beasts and
> Birds of prey
> Just because he follows the Tao,
> Then he's not as smart
> As he'd like you
> To think he is.
> Heck, that's like saying
> We're safe from terrorism
> Just because we follow the Tao.
> Well, given a choice between
> A gas mask and the Tao,
> I'll take the mask.

The infant's virile member may be excited, showing the perfection of its physical essence.

> I don't know about China,
> But in Texas we don't
> Talk about the "virile member"
> Of little boy infants.

56

He who knows the Tao does not care to speak about it; he who speaks about it does not know it.

Trying to understand the Tao
Is like trying to find
Osama bin Laden.
Whoever talks about him
Doesn't know him,
And whoever knows him
Doesn't talk about him.
But that's OK.
We'll hunt those outlaws down.
We'll bring 'em to justice.
That is the American
Way.

57

The multiplication of prohibitive enactments increases the poverty of the people.

> Well, you see?
> Poverty is not my fault.
> It is the fault of Congress
> For making all those
> Laws and regulations.

A sage has said, "I will do nothing and the people will become rich."

> So the Tao says that
> If I have a hands off policy
> Toward the people
> Then they will prosper.
> Well, if things get worse
> With the economy,
> Don't blame me,
> Blame the Tao.

58

The government that seems the most unwise, oft good things to the people supplies; too much meddling, touching everything, will often disappointments bring.

I can go along with this.
We've got to get government
Out of the lives of
The American people.
The people know how
To spend their own money
Better than the government does.
If all this seems unwise,
I don't care.
Take it up with the Tao.

59

There is nothing like moderation.

> I agree,
> There is nothing like moderation,
> But moderation is sometimes good,
> Sometimes bad.
> Good when faced with
> Things like fiscal spending;
> Bad when chasing
> The evildoers.

60

Governing a country is like cooking a fish.

> That's right:
> First catch it,
> Cut the head off,
> Gut it, scale it,
> Rinse it; then
> Fry it, broil it
> Or grill it.
> The point is,
> It's a lot of work,
> And we use a lot
> Of energy.
> It doesn't matter
> Which kind of
> Energy we use,
> But if we don't tap into
> Those oil reserves up in Alaska,
> Some of the fish won't get cooked.
>
> Also, as with #59,
> Cooking a fish is another case
> When you don't want moderation.

61

The great state must learn to abase itself.

Just when I think
The Tao is making sense,
It goes and throws
A passage like this one at us,
Telling us we must learn
To abase ourselves.
Well, America is a great state,
And we're not going to
Abase ourselves before anyone.
No, we're standing tall,
Talking softly,
And don't forget about
That big stick
I spoke of earlier.

62

Why was it the ancients prized this Tao so much; the reason why all under heaven considered it the most valuable thing?

> You know, East is East
> And West is West,
> And they'll forever
> Remain far apart.
> In the East, in China
> They worship the Tao
> As their salvation.
> Out West, in Texas,
> We worship God
> And Jesus.
> Out West, we think
> Jesus is the most valuable
> Thing under heaven,
> And take it from me,
> That's not going to change.

63

It is the way of the Tao to conduct affairs without feeling the trouble of them.

This is what happened
With us in Iraq.
We saw a tyrant who
Needed to be toppled,
So we went in
And toppled him,
Never thinking about
The trouble involved.
Heck, trouble's
Our middle name,
Or one of our names, anyway.
We'll never shy away
From trouble,
'Cause if you don't
Face trouble in
The light of day,
You'll have to face it
In the dark of night.
I like to sleep at night.

64

That which is brittle is easily broken. That which is small is easily dispersed.

Al Qaeda is not small anymore.
At one time it may have been easy
To break them, but that was before
I became President.
I've done a good job
Of dispersing them though.
They couldn't cluster around under
All those bombs we dropped
In Afghanistan.
So they've been dispersed,
And they're pretty brittle now too.
But we've got to keep it up,
And take the fight to them
If we're going to break them for good
And get me re-elected next time.

65

The difficulty in governing the people arises from their having too much knowledge.

I've often thought this was true.
So I've never really wanted
To tell the people very much.
Sometimes when you don't, though,
They end up finding out anyway,
Like when they discovered how
We edited that EPA report.
Nothing much happened,
Of course; it was just a bunch
Of bad publicity for awhile.
I don't care about bad publicity.
I think the people will vote for me
No matter what the press says about me,
Especially as long as I say
We're still at war.

66

The sea is able to receive tribute from all the valley streams because it is lower than they.

There is a big difference
Between the Tao and me.
The Tao relies greatly on
Water images and abasement.
I rely on muscle.
With enough muscle
You can make the water flow
Wherever you want to,
Like with the Panama Canal.
I still hate that we
Had to give that up.

67

I have three precious things which I prize and hold fast: gentleness, economy and shrinking from taking precedence of others

I have three precious things too:
Truth, Justice and the American Way.

Three more things:
The code of the West,
Having a good dog,
And going to church regular.

I could go on with many more,
But you get the idea.

68

He who fights with most good will, to rage makes no resort.

> Good will?
> I've got nothing against
> The Iraqi people.
> I've got nothing against
> Arabs at all,
> Except for those who
> Blew up our Twin Towers,
> Took a big chunk
> Out of the Pentagon,
> And who continue to plot
> Against us.
> Those were acts of war.
> All I've got to say is
> Don't start something
> You can't finish,
> 'Cause we'll finish it for you.
> Otherwise, I'm pursuing
> The war on terrorism calmly,
> Without rage, and with the utmost of
> Good will,
> Even for the French.

69

There is no calamity greater than lightly engaging in war.

Excuse me, I beg to differ.
It would be a greater calamity
If you were against
The United States,
Either as an enemy,
Someone helping the enemy,
Or just as some
Misguided nitwit
Who's always got to pick
The wrong side of every cause,
Like those Taliban guys
We captured in Afghanistan.
We all know where they are now,
Don't we?

70

My words are easy to know and easy to practice; but there is no one in the world who is able to know and able to practice them.

> I can't figure out
> What the heck
> To say about
> This passage.

71

To know and yet to think we do not know is the highest attainment; not to know and yet to think we do know is a disease.

Once again I'm speechless.

72

When people do not fear what they ought to fear, that which is their great dread will come to them.

I think that's what
Happened on 9/11.
We weren't prepared,
And so we got hit.
I'm not sure I would use
The word "fear" so much.
We weren't "alert"
To what we ought to fear.
Well we're alert now.
And we're on alert,
Sometimes orange,
Sometimes red.
I don't like yellow alert.
We're not yellow.
Never were,
Never will be.
I think we need to find another color
For that.

73

It is the way of Heaven not to strive, and yet to skillfully overcome.

That may be OK for Heaven,
But in the real world,
Today's world,
That attitude
Will get you left behind;
If not worse, dead.
Striving is at the
Cornerstone of everything
We hold dear.
You can bet your boots
That other people and
Other countries are
Out there striving.
That's one thing that
Makes America great:
We're better strivers than
Anyone in the world.
Let's keep up the good work!
Go, USA!

74

The people do not fear death. Why try to frighten them? If people always feared death, who would dare to do wrong?

This seems to be an argument
Against capital punishment.
Believe me, I've heard them all.
Well, you've got to be tough
With criminals
Because they're tough.
When I was governor of Texas,
I sent a lot of guilty people
To the Great Hereafter.
They may not have feared
Death in Texas,
But they feared me
Because I was no nonsense.
Don't believe me?
Just try me.

75

The people suffer from famine because of the multitude of taxes consumed by their superiors.

Well, I hate to say
I told you so,
But I told you so.
Let's have another tax cut.

76

What is firm and strong is below, and what is soft and weak is above.

Here we go with the
Weak sister stuff again.
Well, there are no
Weak sisters around here,
And no room for any either.
Just ask Pfc. Jessica Lynch,
A hero in every respect
And in no way weak.
Go ahead, ask her.

77

May not the Way (or Tao) of Heaven be compared to the bending of a bow?

Oh, so "Tao" means "Way."
Interesting,
As in the Frank Sinatra song,
"I Did It My Tao."
Or the Burt Bacharach song,
"Do You Know The Tao To San Jose?"
Or the expression, "No tao, Jose!"

I don't like it.
It doesn't sound right.
They should change
The name of this thing,
Make it so Americans
Can understand it.

78

There is nothing more soft and weak than water; yet for attacking things, nothing can take precedence of it.

Water again!
What is this,
Chinatown the movie?
I drink a lot of water,
Take plenty of showers,
Wash the dogs,
Water the lawn.
Someone else does the dishes
And the windows.
If I want to blow up
A military target,
I'll use a Stealth Bomber
Not a garden hose.

79

When a reconciliation is effected between two parties after a great animosity, there is sure to be a grudge remaining.

I don't have anything
Against the French
After our animosity.
The French Mind is like
The Chinese Mind:
You can't figure it out sometimes.
So I don't hold a grudge.
Heck, I never liked them
Much to begin with.
That hasn't changed.

80

I would make the people return to the use of knotted cords instead of the written characters.

> I hope they don't still
> Have this attitude in China.
> It's kind of hard to sell
> Cell phones, TVs and
> Automobiles to people who
> Are still living in
> The nineteenth century
> B. C.!
>
> I want a better life
> For everyone.
> One hand washes the other,
> To use a little water imagery here.
> You buy our stuff,
> We all benefit.

81

Sincere words are not fine; fine words are not sincere.

Whew!
I'm glad I'm done with
This *Tao Te Ching*
Thing!
I agreed with some of it
And some of it I didn't.
I just wish they'd
Fix the spelling and
Pronunciation of their words,
As fine and sincere
As they may be.
After all, it's not
Hao nao braon cao;
And it's not
The Tow Jones Industrial Average.
Come on guys,
Get with the plan.
You know English is
The world's language
Or should be.

Conclusion

Reading the *Tao Te Ching* and making comments on its verses was challenging and tedious for the President at best, touch and go at worst. He was only able to persevere with a steady diet of peanut butter sandwiches and milk, not to mention various forays onto the campaign trail to raise money for his re-election. When his vacation was over and he had finished reading the *Tao Te Ching*, with a little help, no doubt, from Dr. Rice and others, he had less respect for the Oriental mind than he had to begin with, and he felt better justified in going out and telling the Pacific Rim countries what to do.

0-595-29883-4

www.ingramcontent.com/pod-product-compliance
Lightning Source LLC
Chambersburg PA
CBHW031259280526
45784CB00004B/1920